Christmas, 1952

It is like the strain
waked in the elders
by Susanna

Love
Gerald

By

WALLACE STEVENS

Harmonium (*1923, 1931, 1947*)
Ideas of Order (*1936*)
The Man with the Blue Guitar (*1937*)
Parts of a World (*1942*)
Transport to Summer (*1947*)
The Auroras of Autumn (*1950*)

These are BORZOI BOOKS, *published in New York by*
ALFRED A. KNOPF

HARMONIUM

Harmonium

WALLACE STEVENS

ALFRED · A · KNOPF

NEW YORK

1950

TO MY WIFE

and Holly

THE POEMS IN THIS BOOK

with the exception of "The Comedian as the Letter C" and a few others, have been published before in Others, Secession, Rogue, The Soil, The Modern School, Broom, Contact, The New Republic, The Measure, The Little Review, The Dial, *and particularly in* Poetry: a Magazine of Verse, *of Chicago, edited by Harriet Monroe.*

CONTENTS

ix

x

xi

HARMONIUM

Every time the bucks went clattering
Over Oklahoma
A firecat bristled in the way.

Wherever they went,
They went clattering,
Until they swerved
In a swift, circular line
To the right,
Because of the firecat.

Or until they swerved
In a swift, circular line
To the left,
Because of the firecat.

The bucks clattered.

The firecat went leaping,

To the right, to the left,

And

Bristled in the way.

Later, the firecat closed his bright eyes

And slept.

The soul, O ganders, flies beyond the parks
And far beyond the discords of the wind.

A bronze rain from the sun descending marks
The death of summer, which that time endures

Like one who scrawls a listless testament
Of golden quirks and Paphian caricatures,

Bequeathing your white feathers to the moon
And giving your bland motions to the air.

Behold, already on the long parades
The crows anoint the statues with their dirt.

And the soul, O ganders, being lonely, flies
Beyond your chilly chariots, to the skies.

The lilacs wither in the Carolinas.
Already the butterflies flutter above the cabins.
Already the new-born children interpret love
In the voices of mothers.

Timeless mother,
How is it that your aspic nipples
For once vent honey ?

The pine-tree sweetens my body
The white iris beautifies me.

THE PALTRY NUDE
STARTS ON A SPRING VOYAGE

But not on a shell, she starts,
Archaic, for the sea.
But on the first-found weed
She scuds the glitters,
Noiselessly, like one more wave.

She too is discontent
And would have purple stuff upon her arms,
Tired of the salty harbors,
Eager for the brine and bellowing
Of the high interiors of the sea.

The wind speeds her,
Blowing upon her hands

7

And watery back.

She touches the clouds, where she goes

In the circle of her traverse of the sea.

Yet this is meagre play

In the scurry and water-shine,

As her heels foam —

Not as when the goldener nude

Of a later day

Will go, like the centre of sea-green pomp,

In an intenser calm,

Scullion of fate,

Across the spick torrent, ceaselessly,

Upon her irretrievable way.

First Girl

When this yokel comes maundering,

Whetting his hacker,

I shall run before him,

Diffusing the civilest odors

Out of geraniums and unsmelled flowers.

It will check him.

Second Girl

I shall run before him,

Arching cloths besprinkled with colors

As small as fish-eggs.

The threads

Will abash him.

Third Girl

Oh, la . . . le pauvre !

I shall run before him,

With a curious puffing.

He will bend his ear then.

I shall whisper

Heavenly labials in a world of gutturals.

It will undo him.

INFANTA MARINA

Her terrace was the sand
And the palms and the twilight.

She made of the motions of her wrist
The grandiose gestures
Of her thought.

The rumpling of the plumes
Of this creature of the evening
Came to be sleights of sails
Over the sea.

And thus she roamed
In the roamings of her fan,

11

Partaking of the sea,

And of the evening,

As they flowed around

And uttered their subsiding sound.

DOMINATION OF BLACK

At night, by the fire,
The colors of the bushes
And of the fallen leaves,
Repeating themselves,
Turned in the room,
Like the leaves themselves
Turning in the wind.
Yes: but the color of the heavy hemlocks
Came striding.
And I remembered the cry of the peacocks.

The colors of their tails
Were like the leaves themselves
Turning in the wind,
In the twilight wind.

13

They swept over the room,

Just as they flew from the boughs of the
    hemlocks

Down to the ground.

I heard them cry — the peacocks.

Was it a cry against the twilight

Or against the leaves themselves

Turning in the wind,

Turning as the flames

Turned in the fire,

Turning as the tails of the peacocks

Turned in the loud fire,

Loud as the hemlocks

Full of the cry of the peacocks ?

Or was it a cry against the hemlocks ?

Out of the window,

I saw how the planets gathered

Like the leaves themselves

Turning in the wind.

I saw how the night came,

Came striding like the color of the heavy

  hemlocks

I felt afraid.

And I remembered the cry of the peacocks.

THE SNOW MAN

One must have a mind of winter
To regard the frost and the boughs
Of the pine-trees crusted with snow;

And have been cold a long time
To behold the junipers shagged with ice,
The spruces rough in the distant glitter

Of the January sun; and not to think
Of any misery in the sound of the wind,
In the sound of a few leaves,

Which is the sound of the land
Full of the same wind
That is blowing in the same bare place

For the listener, who listens in the snow,

And, nothing himself, beholds

Nothing that is not there and the nothing that is.

Then from their poverty they rose,
From dry catarrhs, and to guitars
They flitted
Through the palace walls.

They flung monotony behind,
Turned from their want, and, nonchalant,
They crowded
The nocturnal halls.

The lacquered loges huddled there
Mumbled zay-zay and a-zay, a-zay.
The moonlight
Fubbed the girandoles.

And the cold dresses that they wore,
In the vapid haze of the window-bays,
Were tranquil
As they leaned and looked

From the window-sills at the alphabets,
At beta b and gamma g,
To study
The canting curlicues

Of heaven and of the heavenly script.
And there they read of marriage-bed.
Ti-lill-o !
And they read right long.

The gaunt guitarists on the strings
Rumbled a-day and a-day, a-day.
The moonlight
Rose on the beachy floors.

How explicit the coiffures became,
The diamond point, the sapphire point,
The sequins
Of the civil fans !

Insinuations of desire,
Puissant speech, alike in each,
Cried quittance
To the wickless halls.

Then from their poverty they rose,
From dry guitars, and to catarrhs
They flitted
Through the palace walls.

The going of the glade-boat
Is like water flowing;

Like water flowing
Through the green saw-grass,
Under the rainbows;

Under the rainbows
That are like birds,
Turning, bedizened,

While the wind still whistles
As kildeer do,

When they rise
At the red turban
Of the boatman.

I

"Mother of heaven, regina of the clouds,
O sceptre of the sun, crown of the moon,
There is not nothing, no, no, never nothing,
Like the clashed edges of two words that kill."
And so I mocked her in magnificent measure.
Or was it that I mocked myself alone ?
I wish that I might be a thinking stone.
The sea of spuming thought foists up again
The radiant bubble that she was.   And then
A deep up-pouring from some saltier well
Within me, bursts its watery syllable.

II

A red bird flies across the golden floor.

It is a red bird that seeks out his choir

Among the choirs of wind and wet and wing.

A torrent will fall from him when he finds.

Shall I uncrumple this much-crumpled thing?

I am a man of fortune greeting heirs;

For it has come that thus I greet the spring.

These choirs of welcome choir for me farewell.

No spring can follow past meridian.

Yet you persist with anecdotal bliss

To make believe a starry *connaissance*.

III

Is it for nothing, then, that old Chinese

Sat tittivating by their mountain pools

Or in the Yangtse studied out their beards?

I shall not play the flat historic scale.

You know how Utamaro's beauties sought

The end of love in their all-speaking braids.

You know the mountainous coiffures of Bath.

Alas !   Have all the barbers lived in vain

That not one curl in nature has survived ?

Why, without pity on these studious ghosts,

Do you come dripping in your hair from sleep ?

IV

This luscious and impeccable fruit of life

Falls, it appears, of its own weight to earth.

When you were Eve, its acrid juice was sweet,

Untasted, in its heavenly, orchard air.

An apple serves as well as any skull

To be the book in which to read a round,

And is as excellent, in that it is composed

Of what, like skulls, comes rotting back to ground.

But it excels in this, that as the fruit

Of love, it is a book too mad to read

Before one merely reads to pass the time.

V

In the high west there burns a furious star.

It is for fiery boys that star was set

And for sweet-smelling virgins close to them.

The measure of the intensity of love

Is measure, also, of the verve of earth.

For me, the firefly's quick, electric stroke

Ticks tediously the time of one more year.

And you ? Remember how the crickets came

Out of their mother grass, like little kin,

In the pale nights, when your first imagery

Found inklings of your bond to all that dust.

VI

If men at forty will be painting lakes

The ephemeral blues must merge for them in one,

The basic slate, the universal hue.

There is a substance in us that prevails.

But in our amours amorists discern

Such fluctuations that their scrivening

Is breathless to attend each quirky turn.

When amorists grow bald, then amours shrink

Into the compass and curriculum

Of introspective exiles, lecturing.

It is a theme for Hyacinth alone.

VII

The mules that angels ride come slowly down

The blazing passes, from beyond the sun.

Descensions of their tinkling bells arrive.

These muleteers are dainty of their way.

Meantime, centurions guffaw and beat

Their shrilling tankards on the table-boards.

This parable, in sense, amounts to this:

The honey of heaven may or may not come,

But that of earth both comes and goes at once.

Suppose these couriers brought amid their train

A damsel heightened by eternal bloom.

VIII

Like a dull scholar, I behold, in love,

An ancient aspect touching a new mind.

It comes, it blooms, it bears its fruit and dies.

This trivial trope reveals a way of truth.

Our bloom is gone.   We are the fruit thereof.

Two golden gourds distended on our vines,

Into the autumn weather, splashed with frost,

Distorted by hale fatness, turned grotesque.

We hang like warty squashes, streaked and rayed,

The laughing sky will see the two of us

Washed into rinds by rotting winter rains.

IX

In verses wild with motion, full of din,

Loudened by cries, by clashes, quick and sure

As the deadly thought of men accomplishing

Their curious fates in war, come, celebrate

The faith of forty, ward of Cupido.

Most venerable heart, the lustiest conceit

27

Is not too lusty for your broadening.
I quiz all sounds, all thoughts, all everything
For the music and manner of the paladins
To make oblation fit.   Where shall I find
Bravura adequate to this great hymn ?

X

The fops of fancy in their poems leave
Memorabilia of the mystic spouts,
Spontaneously watering their gritty soils.
I am a yeoman, as such fellows go.
I know no magic trees, no balmy boughs,
No silver-ruddy, gold-vermilion fruits.
But, after all, I know a tree that bears
A semblance to the thing I have in mind.
It stands gigantic, with a certain tip
To which all birds come sometime in their time.
But when they go that tip still tips the tree.

XI

If sex were all, then every trembling hand
Could make us squeak, like dolls, the wished-for words.
But note the unconscionable treachery of fate,
That makes us weep, laugh, grunt and groan, and shout
Doleful heroics, pinching gestures forth
From madness or delight, without regard
To that first, foremost law.   Anguishing hour !
Last night, we sat beside a pool of pink,
Clippered with lilies scudding the bright chromes,
Keen to the point of starlight, while a frog
Boomed from his very belly odious chords.

XII

A blue pigeon it is, that circles the blue sky,
On sidelong wing, around and round and round.
A white pigeon it is, that flutters to the ground,
Grown tired of flight.   Like a dark rabbi, I
Observed, when young, the nature of mankind,
In lordly study.   Every day, I found

Man proved a gobbet in my mincing world.

Like a rose rabbi, later, I pursued,

And still pursue, the origin and course

Of love, but until now I never knew

That fluttering things have so distinct a shade.

It's a strange courage
you give me, ancient star:

Shine alone in the sunrise
toward which you lend no part!

I

Shine alone, shine nakedly, shine like bronze,

that reflects neither my face nor any inner part

of my being, shine like fire, that mirrors nothing.

II

Lend no part to any humanity that suffuses

you in its own light.

Be not chimera of morning,

Half-man, half-star.

31

Be not an intelligence,
Like a widow's bird
Or an old horse.

Twenty men crossing a bridge,

Into a village,

Are twenty men crossing twenty bridges,

Into twenty villages,

Or one man

Crossing a single bridge into a village.

This is old song

That will not declare itself . . .

Twenty men crossing a bridge,

Into a village,

Are

Twenty men crossing a bridge

Into a village.

33

That will not declare itself
Yet is certain as meaning . . .

The boots of the men clump
On the boards of the bridge.
The first white wall of the village
Rises through fruit-trees.
Of what was it I was thinking ?
So the meaning escapes.

The first white wall of the village . . .
The fruit-trees. . . .

The white cock's tail
Tosses in the wind.
The turkey-cock's tail
Glitters in the sun.

Water in the fields.
The wind pours down.
The feathers flare
And bluster in the wind.

Remus, blow your horn !
I'm ploughing on Sunday,
Ploughing North America.
Blow your horn !

Tum-ti-tum,
Ti-tum-tum-tum !
The turkey-cock's tail
Spreads to the sun.

The white cock's tail
Streams to the moon.
Water in the fields.
The wind pours down.

Ursula, in a garden, found
A bed of radishes.
She kneeled upon the ground
And gathered them,
With flowers around,
Blue, gold, pink, and green.

She dressed in red and gold brocade
And in the grass an offering made
Of radishes and flowers.

She said, "My dear,
Upon your altars,
I have placed

37

The marguerite and coquelicot,

And roses

Frail as April snow;

But here," she said,

"Where none can see,

I make an offering, in the grass,

Of radishes and flowers."

And then she wept

For fear the Lord would not accept.

The good Lord in His garden sought

New leaf and shadowy tinct,

And they were all His thought.

He heard her low accord,

Half prayer and half ditty,

And He felt a subtle quiver,

That was not heavenly love,

Or pity.

This is not writ

In any book.

I say now, Fernando, that on that day
The mind roamed as a moth roams,
Among the blooms beyond the open sand;

And that whatever noise the motion of the waves
Made on the sea-weeds and the covered stones
Disturbed not even the most idle ear.

Then it was that that monstered moth
Which had lain folded against the blue
And the colored purple of the lazy sea,

And which had drowsed along the bony shores,
Shut to the blather that the water made,
Rose up besprent and sought the flaming red

39

Dabbled with yellow pollen — red as red
As the flag above the old café —
And roamed there all the stupid afternoon.

Barque of phosphor
On the palmy beach,

Move outward into heaven,
Into the alabasters
And night blues.

Foam and cloud are one.
Sultry moon-monsters
Are dissolving.

Fill your black hull
With white moonlight.

There will never be an end
To this droning of the surf.

The doctor of Geneva stamped the sand
That lay impounding the Pacific swell,
Patted his stove-pipe hat and tugged his shawl.

Lacustrine man had never been assailed
By such long-rolling opulent cataracts,
Unless Racine or Bossuet held the like.

He did not quail.   A man so used to plumb
The multifarious heavens felt no awe
Before these visible, voluble delugings,

Which yet found means to set his simmering mind
Spinning and hissing with oracular
Notations of the wild, the ruinous waste,

Until the steeples of his city clanked and sprang
In an unburgherly apocalypse.
The doctor used his handkerchief and sighed.

Pour the unhappiness out
From your too bitter heart,
Which grieving will not sweeten.

Poison grows in this dark.
It is in the water of tears
Its black blooms rise.

The magnificent cause of being,
The imagination, the one reality
In this imagined world

Leaves you
With him for whom no phantasy moves,
And you are pierced by a death.

In the sea, Biscayne, there prinks
The young emerald, evening star,
Good light for drunkards, poets, widows,
And ladies soon to be married.

By this light the salty fishes
Arch in the sea like tree-branches,
Going in many directions
Up and down.

This light conducts
The thoughts of drunkards, the feelings
Of widows and trembling ladies,
The movements of fishes.

45

How pleasant an existence it is
That this emerald charms philosophers,
Until they become thoughtlessly willing
To bathe their hearts in later moonlight,

Knowing that they can bring back thought
In the night that is still to be silent,
Reflecting this thing and that,
Before they sleep !

It is better that, as scholars,
They should think hard in the dark cuffs
Of voluminous cloaks,
And shave their heads and bodies.

It might well be that their mistress
Is no gaunt fugitive phantom.
She might, after all, be a wanton,
Abundantly beautiful, eager,

Fecund,

From whose being by starlight, on sea-coast,

The innermost good of their seeking

Might come in the simplest of speech.

It is a good light, then, for those

That know the ultimate Plato,

Tranquillizing with this jewel

The torments of confusion.

I

The World without Imagination

Nota: man is the intelligence of his soil,
The sovereign ghost.   As such, the Socrates
Of snails, musician of pears, principium
And lex.   Sed quæritur: is this same wig
Of things, this nincompated pedagogue,
Preceptor to the sea ?   Crispin at sea
Created, in his day, a touch of doubt.
An eye most apt in gelatines and jupes,
Berries of villages, a barber's eye,
An eye of land, of simple salad-beds,
Of honest quilts, the eye of Crispin, hung
On porpoises, instead of apricots,
And on silentious porpoises, whose snouts

48

Dibbled in waves that were mustachios,
Inscrutable hair in an inscrutable world.

One eats one paté, even of salt, quotha.
It was not so much the lost terrestrial,
The snug hibernal from that sea and salt,
That century of wind in a single puff.
What counted was mythology of self,
Blotched out beyond unblotching.   Crispin,
The lutanist of fleas, the knave, the thane,
The ribboned stick, the bellowing breeches, cloak
Of China, cap of Spain, imperative haw
Of hum, inquisitorial botanist,
And general lexicographer of mute
And maidenly greenhorns, now beheld himself,
A skinny sailor peering in the sea-glass.
What word split up in clickering syllables
And storming under multitudinous tones
Was name for this short-shanks in all that brunt ?
Crispin was washed away by magnitude.

The whole of life that still remained in him
Dwindled to one sound strumming in his ear,
Ubiquitous concussion, slap and sigh,
Polyphony beyond his baton's thrust.

Could Crispin stem verboseness in the sea,
The old age of a watery realist,
Triton, dissolved in shifting diaphanes
Of blue and green ?   A wordy, watery age
That whispered to the sun's compassion, made
A convocation, nightly, of the sea-stars,
And on the clopping foot-ways of the moon
Lay grovelling.   Triton incomplicate with that
Which made him Triton, nothing left of him,
Except in faint, memorial gesturings,
That were like arms and shoulders in the waves,
Here, something in the rise and fall of wind
That seemed hallucinating horn, and here,
A sunken voice, both of remembering
And of forgetfulness, in alternate strain.

Just so an ancient Crispin was dissolved.

The valet in the tempest was annulled.

Bordeaux to Yucatan, Havana next,

And then to Carolina.   Simple jaunt.

Crispin, merest minuscule in the gales,

Dejected his manner to the turbulence.

The salt hung on his spirit like a frost,

The dead brine melted in him like a dew

Of winter, until nothing of himself

Remained, except some starker, barer self

In a starker, barer world, in which the sun

Was not the sun because it never shone

With bland complaisance on pale parasols,

Beetled, in chapels, on the chaste bouquets.

Against his pipping sounds a trumpet cried

Celestial sneering boisterously.   Crispin

Became an introspective voyager.

Here was the veritable ding an sich, at last,

Crispin confronting it, a vocable thing,

But with a speech belched out of hoary darks
Noway resembling his, a visible thing,
And excepting negligible Triton, free
From the unavoidable shadow of himself
That lay elsewhere around him.   Severance
Was clear.   The last distortion of romance
Forsook the insatiable egotist.   The sea
Severs not only lands but also selves.
Here was no help before reality.
Crispin beheld and Crispin was made new.
The imagination, here, could not evade,
In poems of plums, the strict austerity
Of one vast, subjugating, final tone.
The drenching of stale lives no more fell down.
What was this gaudy, gusty panoply?
Out of what swift destruction did it spring?
It was caparison of wind and cloud
And something given to make whole among
The ruses that were shattered by the large.

Concerning the Thunderstorms of Yucatan

In Yucatan, the Maya sonneteers
Of the Caribbean amphitheatre,
In spite of hawk and falcon, green toucan
And jay, still to the night-bird made their plea,
As if raspberry tanagers in palms,
High up in orange air, were barbarous.
But Crispin was too destitute to find
In any commonplace the sought-for aid.
He was a man made vivid by the sea,
A man come out of luminous traversing,
Much trumpeted, made desperately clear,
Fresh from discoveries of tidal skies,
To whom oracular rockings gave no rest.
Into a savage color he went on.

How greatly had he grown in his demesne,
This auditor of insects !   He that saw
The stride of vanishing autumn in a park

By way of decorous melancholy; he
That wrote his couplet yearly to the spring,
As dissertation of profound delight,
Stopping, on voyage, in a land of snakes,
Found his vicissitudes had much enlarged
His apprehension, made him intricate
In moody rucks, and difficult and strange
In all desires, his destitution's mark.
He was in this as other freemen are,
Sonorous nutshells rattling inwardly.
His violence was for aggrandizement
And not for stupor, such as music makes
For sleepers halfway waking.   He perceived
That coolness for his heat came suddenly,
And only, in the fables that he scrawled
With his own quill, in its indigenous dew,
Of an æsthetic tough, diverse, untamed,
Incredible to prudes, the mint of dirt,
Green barbarism turning paradigm.
Crispin foresaw a curious promenade

Or, nobler, sensed an elemental fate,

And elemental potencies and pangs,

And beautiful barenesses as yet unseen,

Making the most of savagery of palms,

Of moonlight on the thick, cadaverous bloom

That yuccas breed, and of the panther's tread.

The fabulous and its intrinsic verse

Came like two spirits parleying, adorned

In radiance from the Atlantic coign,

For Crispin and his quill to catechize.

But they came parleying of such an earth,

So thick with sides and jagged lops of green,

So intertwined with serpent-kin encoiled

Among the purple tufts, the scarlet crowns,

Scenting the jungle in their refuges,

So streaked with yellow, blue and green and red

In beak and bud and fruity gobbet-skins,

That earth was like a jostling festival

Of seeds grown fat, too juicily opulent,

Expanding in the gold's maternal warmth.

So much for that.   The affectionate emigrant found
A new reality in parrot-squawks.
Yet let that trifle pass.   Now, as this odd
Discoverer walked through the harbor streets
Inspecting the cabildo, the façade
Of the cathedral, making notes, he heard
A rumbling, west of Mexico, it seemed,
Approaching like a gasconade of drums.
The white cabildo darkened, the façade,
As sullen as the sky, was swallowed up
In swift, successive shadows, dolefully.
The rumbling broadened as it fell.   The wind,
Tempestuous clarion, with heavy cry,
Came bluntly thundering, more terrible
Than the revenge of music on bassoons.
Gesticulating lightning, mystical,
Made pallid flitter.   Crispin, here, took flight.
An annotator has his scruples, too.
He knelt in the cathedral with the rest,
This connoisseur of elemental fate,

Aware of exquisite thought.   The storm was one
Of many proclamations of the kind,
Proclaiming something harsher than he learned
From hearing signboards whimper in cold nights
Or seeing the midsummer artifice
Of heat upon his pane.   This was the span
Of force, the quintessential fact, the note
Of Vulcan, that a valet seeks to own,
The thing that makes him envious in phrase.

And while the torrent on the roof still droned
He felt the Andean breath.   His mind was free
And more than free, elate, intent, profound
And studious of a self possessing him,
That was not in him in the crusty town
From which he sailed.   Beyond him, westward, lay
The mountainous ridges, purple balustrades,
In which the thunder, lapsing in its clap,
Let down gigantic quavers of its voice,
For Crispin to vociferate again.

III

Approaching Carolina

The book of moonlight is not written yet
Nor half begun, but, when it is, leave room
For Crispin, fagot in the lunar fire,
Who, in the hubbub of his pilgrimage
Through sweating changes, never could forget
That wakefulness or meditating sleep,
In which the sulky strophes willingly
Bore up, in time, the somnolent, deep songs.
Leave room, therefore, in that unwritten book
For the legendary moonlight that once burned
In Crispin's mind above a continent.
America was always north to him,
A northern west or western north, but north,
And thereby polar, polar-purple, chilled
And lank, rising and slumping from a sea
Of hardy foam, receding flatly, spread
In endless ledges, glittering, submerged

And cold in a boreal mistiness of the moon.
The spring came there in clinking pannicles
Of half-dissolving frost, the summer came,
If ever, whisked and wet, not ripening,
Before the winter's vacancy returned.
The myrtle, if the myrtle ever bloomed,
Was like a glacial pink upon the air.
The green palmettoes in crepuscular ice
Clipped frigidly blue-black meridians,
Morose chiaroscuro, gauntly drawn.

How many poems he denied himself
In his observant progress, lesser things
Than the relentless contact he desired;
How many sea-masks he ignored; what sounds
He shut out from his tempering ear; what thoughts,
Like jades affecting the sequestered bride;
And what descants, he sent to banishment !
Perhaps the Arctic moonlight really gave
The liaison, the blissful liaison,

Between himself and his environment,
Which was, and is, chief motive, first delight,
For him, and not for him alone.   It seemed
Illusive, faint, more mist than moon, perverse,
Wrong as a divagation to Peking,
To him that postulated as his theme
The vulgar, as his theme and hymn and flight,
A passionately niggling nightingale.
Moonlight was an evasion, or, if not,
A minor meeting, facile, delicate.

Thus he conceived his voyaging to be
An up and down between two elements,
A fluctuating between sun and moon,
A sally into gold and crimson forms,
As on this voyage, out of goblinry,
And then retirement like a turning back
And sinking down to the indulgences
That in the moonlight have their habitude.
But let these backward lapses, if they would,

Grind their seductions on him, Crispin knew
It was a flourishing tropic he required
For his refreshment, an abundant zone,
Prickly and obdurate, dense, harmonious,
Yet with a harmony not rarefied
Nor fined for the inhibited instruments
Of over-civil stops.   And thus he tossed
Between a Carolina of old time,
A little juvenile, an ancient whim,
And the visible, circumspect presentment drawn
From what he saw across his vessel's prow.

He came.   The poetic hero without palms
Or jugglery, without regalia.
And as he came he saw that it was spring,
A time abhorrent to the nihilist
Or searcher for the fecund minimum.
The moonlight fiction disappeared.   The spring,
Although contending featly in its veils,
Irised in dew and early fragrancies,

Was gemmy marionette to him that sought
A sinewy nakedness.   A river bore
The vessel inward.   Tilting up his nose,
He inhaled the rancid rosin, burly smells
Of dampened lumber, emanations blown
From warehouse doors, the gustiness of ropes,
Decays of sacks, and all the arrant stinks
That helped him round his rude æsthetic out.
He savored rankness like a sensualist.
He marked the marshy ground around the dock,
The crawling railroad spur, the rotten fence,
Curriculum for the marvelous sophomore.
It purified.   It made him see how much
Of what he saw he never saw at all.
He gripped more closely the essential prose
As being, in a world so falsified,
The one integrity for him, the one
Discovery still possible to make,
To which all poems were incident, unless
That prose should wear a poem's guise at last.

The Idea of a Colony

Nota: his soil is man's intelligence.

That's better.   That's worth crossing seas to find.

Crispin in one laconic phrase laid bare

His cloudy drift and planned a colony.

Exit the mental moonlight, exit lex,

Rex and principium, exit the whole

Shebang.   Exeunt omnes.   Here was prose

More exquisite than any tumbling verse:

A still new continent in which to dwell.

What was the purpose of his pilgrimage,

Whatever shape it took in Crispin's mind,

If not, when all is said, to drive away

The shadow of his fellows from the skies,

And, from their stale intelligence released,

To make a new intelligence prevail ?

Hence the reverberations in the words

Of his first central hymns, the celebrants

Of rankest trivia, tests of the strength
Of his æsthetic, his philosophy,
The more invidious, the more desired.
The florist asking aid from cabbages,
The rich man going bare, the paladin
Afraid, the blind man as astronomer,
The appointed power unwielded from disdain.
His western voyage ended and began.
The torment of fastidious thought grew slack,
Another, still more bellicose, came on.
He, therefore, wrote his prolegomena,
And, being full of the caprice, inscribed
Commingled souvenirs and prophecies.
He made a singular collation.   Thus:
The natives of the rain are rainy men.
Although they paint effulgent, azure lakes,
And April hillsides wooded white and pink,
Their azure has a cloudy edge, their white
And pink, the water bright that dogwood bears.
And in their music showering sounds intone.

On what strange froth does the gross Indian dote,

What Eden sapling gum, what honeyed gore,

What pulpy dram distilled of innocence,

That streaking gold should speak in him

Or bask within his images and words ?

If these rude instances impeach themselves

By force of rudeness, let the principle

Be plain.   For application Crispin strove,

Abhorring Turk as Esquimau, the lute

As the marimba, the magnolia as rose.

Upon these premises propounding, he

Projected a colony that should extend

To the dusk of a whistling south below the south,

A comprehensive island hemisphere.

The man in Georgia waking among pines

Should be pine-spokesman.   The responsive man,

Planting his pristine cores in Florida,

Should prick thereof, not on the psaltery,

But on the banjo's categorical gut,

Tuck, tuck, while the flamingoes flapped his bays.

Sepulchral señors, bibbling pale mescal,

Oblivious to the Aztec almanacs,

Should make the intricate Sierra scan.

And dark Brazilians in their cafés,

Musing immaculate, pampean dits,

Should scrawl a vigilant anthology,

To be their latest, lucent paramour.

These are the broadest instances.   Crispin,

Progenitor of such extensive scope,

Was not indifferent to smart detail.

The melon should have apposite ritual,

Performed in verd apparel, and the peach,

When its black branches came to bud, belle day,

Should have an incantation.   And again,

When piled on salvers its aroma steeped

The summer, it should have a sacrament

And celebration.   Shrewd novitiates

Should be the clerks of our experience.

These bland excursions into time to come,

Related in romance to backward flights,

However prodigal, however proud,

Contained in their afflatus the reproach

That first drove Crispin to his wandering.

He could not be content with counterfeit,

With masquerade of thought, with hapless words

That must belie the racking masquerade,

With fictive flourishes that preordained

His passion's permit, hang of coat, degree

Of buttons, measure of his salt.   Such trash

Might help the blind, not him, serenely sly.

It irked beyond his patience.   Hence it was,

Preferring text to gloss, he humbly served

Grotesque apprenticeship to chance event,

A clown, perhaps, but an aspiring clown.

There is a monotonous babbling in our dreams

That makes them our dependent heirs, the heirs

Of dreamers buried in our sleep, and not

The oncoming fantasies of better birth.

The apprentice knew these dreamers.   If he dreamed
Their dreams, he did it in a gingerly way.
All dreams are vexing.   Let them be expunged.
But let the rabbit run, the cock declaim.

Trinket pasticcio, flaunting skyey sheets,
With Crispin as the tiptoe cozener ?
No, no: veracious page on page, exact.

v

A Nice Shady Home

Crispin as hermit, pure and capable,
Dwelt in the land.   Perhaps if discontent
Had kept him still the pricking realist,
Choosing his element from droll confect
Of was and is and shall or ought to be,
Beyond Bordeaux, beyond Havana, far
Beyond carked Yucatan, he might have come
To colonize his polar planterdom
And jig his chits upon a cloudy knee.

68

But his emprize to that idea soon sped.

Crispin dwelt in the land and dwelling there

Slid from his continent by slow recess

To things within his actual eye, alert

To the difficulty of rebellious thought

When the sky is blue.   The blue infected will.

It may be that the yarrow in his fields

Sealed pensive purple under its concern.

But day by day, now this thing and now that

Confined him, while it cosseted, condoned,

Little by little, as if the suzerain soil

Abashed him by carouse to humble yet

Attach.   It seemed haphazard denouement.

He first, as realist, admitted that

Whoever hunts a matinal continent

May, after all, stop short before a plum

And be content and still be realist.

The words of things entangle and confuse.

The plum survives its poems.   It may hang

In the sunshine placidly, colored by ground

Obliquities of those who pass beneath,

Harlequined and mazily dewed and mauved

In bloom.   Yet it survives in its own form,

Beyond these changes, good, fat, guzzly fruit.

So Crispin hasped on the surviving form,

For him, of shall or ought to be in is.

Was he to bray this in profoundest brass

Arointing his dreams with fugal requiems?

Was he to company vastest things defunct

With a blubber of tom-toms harrowing the sky?

Scrawl a tragedian's testament?   Prolong

His active force in an inactive dirge,

Which, let the tall musicians call and call,

Should merely call him dead?   Pronounce amen

Through choirs infolded to the outmost clouds?

Because he built a cabin who once planned

Loquacious columns by the ructive sea?

Because he turned to salad-beds again?

Jovial Crispin, in calamitous crape?

Should he lay by the personal and make

Of his own fate an instance of all fate?

What is one man among so many men?

What are so many men in such a world?

Can one man think one thing and think it long?

Can one man be one thing and be it long?

The very man despising honest quilts

Lies quilted to his poll in his despite.

For realists, what is is what should be.

And so it came, his cabin shuffled up,

His trees were planted, his duenna brought

Her prismy blonde and clapped her in his hands,

The curtains flittered and the door was closed.

Crispin, magister of a single room,

Latched up the night. So deep a sound fell down

It was as if the solitude concealed

And covered him and his congenial sleep.

So deep a sound fell down it grew to be

A long soothsaying silence down and down.

The crickets beat their tambours in the wind,
Marching a motionless march, custodians.

In the presto of the morning, Crispin trod,
Each day, still curious, but in a round
Less prickly and much more condign than that
He once thought necessary.   Like Candide,
Yeoman and grub, but with a fig in sight,
And cream for the fig and silver for the cream,
A blonde to tip the silver and to taste
The rapey gouts.   Good star, how that to be
Annealed them in their cabin ribaldries !
Yet the quotidian saps philosophers
And men like Crispin like them in intent,
If not in will, to track the knaves of thought.
But the quotidian composed as his,
Of breakfast ribands, fruits laid in their leaves,
The tomtit and the cassia and the rose,
Although the rose was not the noble thorn
Of crinoline spread, but of a pining sweet,

Composed of evenings like cracked shutters flung
Upon the rumpling bottomness, and nights
In which those frail custodians watched,
Indifferent to the tepid summer cold,
While he poured out upon the lips of her
That lay beside him, the quotidian
Like this, saps like the sun, true fortuner.
For all it takes it gives a humped return
Exchequering from piebald fiscs unkeyed.

VI
And Daughters with Curls

Portentous enunciation, syllable
To blessed syllable affined, and sound
Bubbling felicity in cantilene,
Prolific and tormenting tenderness
Of music, as it comes to unison,
Forgather and bell boldly Crispin's last
Deduction.   Thrum with a proud douceur
His grand pronunciamento and devise.

73

The chits came for his jigging, bluet-eyed,

Hands without touch yet touching poignantly,

Leaving no room upon his cloudy knee,

Prophetic joint, for its diviner young.

The return to social nature, once begun,

Anabasis or slump, ascent or chute,

Involved him in midwifery so dense

His cabin counted as phylactery,

Then place of vexing palankeens, then haunt

Of children nibbling at the sugared void,

Infants yet eminently old, then dome

And halidom for the unbraided femes,

Green crammers of the green fruits of the world,

Bidders and biders for its ecstasies,

True daughters both of Crispin and his clay.

All this with many mulctings of the man,

Effective colonizer sharply stopped

In the door-yard by his own capacious bloom.

But that this bloom grown riper, showing nibs

Of its eventual roundness, puerile tints

Of spiced and weathery rouges, should complex

The stopper to indulgent fatalist

Was unforeseen.   First Crispin smiled upon

His goldenest demoiselle, inhabitant,

She seemed, of a country of the capuchins,

So delicately blushed, so humbly eyed,

Attentive to a coronal of things

Secret and singular.   Second, upon

A second similar counterpart, a maid

Most sisterly to the first, not yet awake

Excepting to the motherly footstep, but

Marvelling sometimes at the shaken sleep.

Then third, a thing still flaxen in the light,

A creeper under jaunty leaves.   And fourth,

Mere blusteriness that gewgaws jollified,

All din and gobble, blasphemously pink.

A few years more and the vermeil capuchin

Gave to the cabin, lordlier than it was,

The dulcet omen fit for such a house.

The second sister dallying was shy

To fetch the one full-pinioned one himself

Out of her botches, hot embosomer.

The third one gaping at the orioles

Lettered herself demurely as became

A pearly poetess, peaked for rhapsody.

The fourth, pent now, a digit curious.

Four daughters in a world too intricate

In the beginning, four blithe instruments

Of differing struts, four voices several

In couch, four more personæ, intimate

As buffo, yet divers, four mirrors blue

That should be silver, four accustomed seeds

Hinting incredible hues, four selfsame lights

That spread chromatics in hilarious dark,

Four questioners and four sure answerers.

Crispin concocted doctrine from the rout.

The world, a turnip once so readily plucked,

Sacked up and carried overseas, daubed out

Of its ancient purple, pruned to the fertile main,

And sown again by the stiffest realist,

Came reproduced in purple, family font,

The same insoluble lump.   The fatalist

Stepped in and dropped the chuckling down his craw,

Without grace or grumble.   Score this anecdote

Invented for its pith, not doctrinal

In form though in design, as Crispin willed,

Disguised pronunciamento, summary,

Autumn's compendium, strident in itself

But muted, mused, and perfectly revolved

In those portentous accents, syllables,

And sounds of music coming to accord

Upon his law, like their inherent sphere,

Seraphic proclamations of the pure

Delivered with a deluging onwardness.

Or if the music sticks, if the anecdote

Is false, if Crispin is a profitless

Philosopher, beginning with green brag,

Concluding fadedly, if as a man

Prone to distemper he abates in taste,

Fickle and fumbling, variable, obscure,

Glozing his life with after-shining flicks,

Illuminating, from a fancy gorged

By apparition, plain and common things,

Sequestering the fluster from the year,

Making gulped potions from obstreperous drops,

And so distorting, proving what he proves

Is nothing, what can all this matter since

The relation comes, benignly, to its end?

So may the relation of each man be clipped.

I have finished my combat with the sun;
And my body, the old animal,
Knows nothing more.

The powerful seasons bred and killed,
And were themselves the genii
Of their own ends.

Oh, but the very self of the storm
Of sun and slaves, breeding and death,
The old animal,

The senses and feeling, the very sound
And sight, and all there was of the storm,
Knows nothing more.

A few things for themselves,

Convolvulus and coral,

Buzzards and live-moss,

Tiestas from the keys,

A few things for themselves,

Florida, venereal soil,

Disclose to the lover.

The dreadful sundry of this world,

The Cuban, Polodowsky,

The Mexican women,

The negro undertaker

Killing the time between corpses

Fishing for crayfish . . .

Virgin of boorish births,

80

Swiftly in the nights,
In the porches of Key West,
Behind the bougainvilleas,
After the guitar is asleep,
Lasciviously as the wind,
You come tormenting,
Insatiable,

When you might sit,
A scholar of darkness,
Sequestered over the sea,
Wearing a clear tiara
Of red and blue and red,
Sparkling, solitary, still,
In the high sea-shadow.

Donna, donna, dark,
Stooping in indigo gown
And cloudy constellations,
Conceal yourself or disclose

81

Fewest things to the lover —
A hand that bears a thick-leaved fruit,
A pungent bloom against your shade.

To what good, in the alleys of the lilacs,
O caliper, do you scratch your buttocks
And tell the divine ingénue, your companion,
That this bloom is the bloom of soap
And this fragrance the fragrance of vegetal?

Do you suppose that she cares a tick,
In this hymeneal air, what it is
That marries her innocence thus,
So that her nakedness is near,
Or that she will pause at scurrilous words?

Poor buffo!   Look at the lavender
And look your last and look still steadily,
And say how it comes that you see

83

Nothing but trash and that you no longer feel
Her body quivering in the Floréal

Toward the cool night and its fantastic star,
Prime paramour and belted paragon,
Well-booted, rugged, arrogantly male,
Patron and imager of the gold Don John,
Who will embrace her before summer comes.

Out of the tomb, we bring Badroulbadour,
Within our bellies, we her chariot.
Here is an eye.   And here are, one by one,
The lashes of that eye and its white lid.
Here is the cheek on which that lid declined,
And, finger after finger, here, the hand,
The genius of that cheek.   Here are the lips,
The bundle of the body and the feet.

.   .   .   .

Out of the tomb we bring Badroulbadour.

THE JACK-RABBIT

In the morning,
The jack-rabbit sang to the Arkansaw.
He carolled in caracoles
On the feat sandbars.

The black man said,
"Now, grandmother,
Crochet me this buzzard
On your winding-sheet,
And do not forget his wry neck
After the winter."

The black man said,
"Look out, O caroller,
The entrails of the buzzard
Are rattling."

VALLEY CANDLE

My candle burned alone in an immense valley.
Beams of the huge night converged upon it,
Until the wind blew.
Then beams of the huge night
Converged upon its image,
Until the wind blew.

ANECDOTE OF MEN BY THE THOUSAND

The soul, he said, is composed
Of the external world.

There are men of the East, he said,
Who are the East.
There are men of a province
Who are that province.
There are men of a valley
Who are that valley.

There are men whose words
Are as natural sounds
Of their places
As the cackle of toucans
In the place of toucans.

The mandoline is the instrument
Of a place.

Are there mandolines of western mountains ?
Are there mandolines of northern moonlight ?

The dress of a woman of Lhassa,
In its place,
Is an invisible element of that place
Made visible.

I

I figured you as nude between
Monotonous earth and dark blue sky.
It made you seem so small and lean
And nameless,
Heavenly Vincentine.

II

I saw you then, as warm as flesh,
Brunette,
But yet not too brunette,
As warm, as clean.
Your dress was green,
Was whited green,
Green Vincentine.

III

Then you came walking,
In a group
Of human others,
Voluble.
Yes: you came walking,
Vincentine.
Yes: you came talking.

IV

And what I knew you felt
Came then.
Monotonous earth I saw become
Illimitable spheres of you,
And that white animal, so lean,
Turned Vincentine,
Turned heavenly Vincentine,
And that white animal, so lean,
Turned heavenly, heavenly Vincentine.

FLORAL DECORATIONS FOR
BANANAS

Well, nuncle, this plainly won't do.
These insolent, linear peels
And sullen, hurricane shapes
Won't do with your eglantine.
They require something serpentine.
Blunt yellow in such a room !

You should have had plums tonight,
In an eighteenth-century dish,
And pettifogging buds,
For the women of primrose and purl,
Each one in her decent curl.
Good God ! What a precious light !

But bananas hacked and hunched . . .
The table was set by an ogre,
His eye on an outdoor gloom
And a stiff and noxious place.
Pile the bananas on planks.
The women will be all shanks
And bangles and slatted eyes.

And deck the bananas in leaves
Plucked from the Carib trees,
Fibrous and dangling down,
Oozing cantankerous gum
Out of their purple maws,
Darting out of their purple craws
Their musky and tingling tongues.

Huge are the canna in the dreams of
X, the mighty thought, the mighty man.
They fill the terrace of his capitol.

His thought sleeps not.   Yet thought that wakes
In sleep may never meet another thought
Or thing. . . . Now day-break comes. . . .

X promenades the dewy stones,
Observes the canna with a clinging eye,
Observes and then continues to observe.

ON THE MANNER OF ADDRESSING
CLOUDS

Gloomy grammarians in golden gowns,

Meekly you keep the mortal rendezvous,

Eliciting the still sustaining pomps

Of speech which are like music so profound

They seem an exaltation without sound.

Funest philosophers and ponderers,

Their evocations are the speech of clouds.

So speech of your processionals returns

In the casual evocations of your tread

Across the stale, mysterious seasons.   These

Are the music of meet resignation; these

The responsive, still sustaining pomps for you

To magnify, if in that drifting waste

You are to be accompanied by more

Than mute bare splendors of the sun and moon.

95

OF HEAVEN CONSIDERED AS A
TOMB

What word have you, interpreters, of men
Who in the tomb of heaven walk by night,
The darkened ghosts of our old comedy ?
Do they believe they range the gusty cold,
With lanterns borne aloft to light the way,
Freemen of death, about and still about
To find whatever it is they seek ?   Or does
That burial, pillared up each day as porte
And spiritous passage into nothingness,
Foretell each night the one abysmal night,
When the host shall no more wander, nor the light
Of the steadfast lanterns creep across the dark ?
Make hue among the dark comedians,
Halloo them in the topmost distances
For answer from their icy Élysée.

I

In my room, the world is beyond my understanding;

But when I walk I see that it consists of three or four

hills and a cloud.

II

From my balcony, I survey the yellow air,

Reading where I have written,

"The spring is like a belle undressing."

III

The gold tree is blue.

The singer has pulled his cloak over his head.

The moon is in the folds of the cloak.

In the moonlight
I met Berserk,
In the moonlight
On the bushy plain.
Oh, sharp he was
As the sleepless !

And, "Why are you red
In this milky blue ?"
I said.
"Why sun-colored,
As if awake
In the midst of sleep ?"

"You that wander,"
So he said,
"On the bushy plain,
Forget so soon.
But I set my traps
In the midst of dreams."

I knew from this
That the blue ground
Was full of blocks
And blocking steel.
I knew the dread
Of the bushy plain,
And the beauty
Of the moonlight
Falling there,
Falling
As sleep falls
In the innocent air.

99

A HIGH-TONED OLD CHRISTIAN
WOMAN

Poetry is the supreme fiction, madame.
Take the moral law and make a nave of it
And from the nave build haunted heaven.   Thus,
The conscience is converted into palms,
Like windy citherns hankering for hymns.
We agree in principle.   That's clear.   But take
The opposing law and make a peristyle,
And from the peristyle project a masque
Beyond the planets.   Thus, our bawdiness,
Unpurged by epitaph, indulged at last,
Is equally converted into palms,
Squiggling like saxophones.   And palm for palm,
Madame, we are where we began.   Allow,
Therefore, that in the planetary scene

Your disaffected flagellants, well-stuffed,

Smacking their muzzy bellies in parade,

Proud of such novelties of the sublime,

Such tink and tank and tunk-a-tunk-tunk,

May, merely may, madame, whip from themselves

A jovial hullabaloo among the spheres.

This will make widows wince.   But fictive things

Wink as they will.   Wink most when widows wince.

Let the place of the solitaires
Be a place of perpetual undulation.

Whether it be in mid-sea
On the dark, green water-wheel,
Or on the beaches,
There must be no cessation
Of motion, or of the noise of motion,
The renewal of noise
And manifold continuation;

And, most, of the motion of thought
And its restless iteration,

In the place of the solitaires,
Which is to be a place of perpetual undulation.

It is with a strange malice
That I distort the world.

Ah ! that ill humors
Should mask as white girls.
And ah ! that Scaramouche
Should have a black barouche.

The sorry verities !
Yet in excess, continual,
There is cure of sorrow.

Permit that if as ghost I come
Among the people burning in me still,
I come as belle design
Of foppish line.

And I, then, tortured for old speech,
A white of wildly woven rings;
I, weeping in a calcined heart,
My hands such sharp, imagined things.

THE CURTAINS IN THE HOUSE
OF THE METAPHYSICIAN

It comes about that the drifting of these curtains
Is full of long motions; as the ponderous
Deflations of distance; or as clouds
Inseparable from their afternoons;
Or the changing of light, the dropping
Of the silence, wide sleep and solitude
Of night, in which all motion
Is beyond us, as the firmament,
Up-rising and down-falling, bares
The last largeness, bold to see.

Two wooden tubs of blue hydrangeas stand at the foot
of the stone steps.

The sky is a blue gum streaked with rose.   The trees
are black.

The grackles crack their throats of bone in the smooth
air.

Moisture and heat have swollen the garden into a slum
of bloom.

Pardie !   Summer is like a fat beast, sleepy in mildew,

Our old bane, green and bloated, serene, who cries,

"That bliss of stars, that princox of evening heaven !"
reminding of seasons,

When radiance came running down, slim through the
bareness.

And so it is one damns that green shade at the bottom
of the land.

For who can care at the wigs despoiling the Satan ear ?

And who does not seek the sky unfuzzed, soaring to the
princox ?

One has a malady, here, a malady.   One feels a malady.

The cock crows
But no queen rises.

The hair of my blonde
Is dazzling,
As the spittle of cows
Threading the wind.

Ho ! Ho !

But ki-ki-ri-ki
Brings no rou-cou,
No rou-cou-cou.

But no queen comes
In slipper green.

Call the roller of big cigars,
The muscular one, and bid him whip
In kitchen cups concupiscent curds.
Let the wenches dawdle in such dress
As they are used to wear, and let the boys
Bring flowers in last month's newspapers.
Let be be finale of seem.
The only emperor is the emperor of ice-cream.

Take from the dresser of deal,
Lacking the three glass knobs, that sheet
On which she embroidered fantails once
And spread it so as to cover her face.
If her horny feet protrude, they come
To show how cold she is, and dumb.
Let the lamp affix its beam.
The only emperor is the emperor of ice-cream.

I went to Egypt to escape
The Indian, but the Indian struck
Out of his cloud and from his sky.

This was no worm bred in the moon,
Wriggling far down the phantom air,
And on a comfortable sofa dreamed.

The Indian struck and disappeared.
I knew my enemy was near — I,
Drowsing in summer's sleepiest horn.

Not less because in purple I descended
The western day through what you called
The loneliest air, not less was I myself.

What was the ointment sprinkled on my beard ?
What were the hymns that buzzed beside my ears ?
What was the sea whose tide swept through me there ?

Out of my mind the golden ointment rained,
And my ears made the blowing hymns they heard.
I was myself the compass of that sea:

I was the world in which I walked, and what I saw
Or heard or felt came not but from myself;
And there I found myself more truly and more strange.

111

The houses are haunted

By white night-gowns.

None are green,

Or purple with green rings,

Or green with yellow rings,

Or yellow with blue rings.

None of them are strange,

With socks of lace

And beaded ceintures.

People are not going

To dream of baboons and periwinkles.

Only, here and there, an old sailor,

Drunk and asleep in his boots,

Catches tigers

In red weather.

SUNDAY MORNING

I

Complacencies of the peignoir, and late
Coffee and oranges in a sunny chair,
And the green freedom of a cockatoo
Upon a rug mingle to dissipate
The holy hush of ancient sacrifice.
She dreams a little, and she feels the dark
Encroachment of that old catastrophe,
As a calm darkens among water-lights.
The pungent oranges and bright, green wings
Seem things in some procession of the dead,
Winding across wide water, without sound.
The day is like wide water, without sound,
Stilled for the passing of her dreaming feet
Over the seas, to silent Palestine,
Dominion of the blood and sepulchre.

II

Why should she give her bounty to the dead ?

What is divinity if it can come

Only in silent shadows and in dreams ?

Shall she not find in comforts of the sun,

In pungent fruit and bright, green wings, or else

In any balm or beauty of the earth,

Things to be cherished like the thought of heaven ?

Divinity must live within herself:

Passions of rain, or moods in falling snow;

Grievings in loneliness, or unsubdued

Elations when the forest blooms; gusty

Emotions on wet roads on autumn nights;

All pleasures and all pains, remembering

The bough of summer and the winter branch.

These are the measures destined for her soul.

III

Jove in the clouds had his inhuman birth.

No mother suckled him, no sweet land gave

Large-mannered motions to his mythy mind
He moved among us, as a muttering king,
Magnificent, would move among his hinds,
Until our blood, commingling, virginal,
With heaven, brought such requital to desire
The very hinds discerned it, in a star.
Shall our blood fail ?   Or shall it come to be
The blood of paradise ?   And shall the earth
Seem all of paradise that we shall know ?
The sky will be much friendlier then than now,
A part of labor and a part of pain,
And next in glory to enduring love,
Not this dividing and indifferent blue.

IV

She says, "I am content when wakened birds,
Before they fly, test the reality
Of misty fields, by their sweet questionings;
But when the birds are gone, and their warm fields
Return no more, where, then, is paradise ?"

There is not any haunt of prophecy,

Nor any old chimera of the grave,

Neither the golden underground, nor isle

Melodious, where spirits gat them home,

Nor visionary south, nor cloudy palm

Remote on heaven's hill, that has endured

As April's green endures; or will endure

Like her remembrance of awakened birds,

Or her desire for June and evening, tipped

By the consummation of the swallow's wings

V

She says, "But in contentment I still feel

The need of some imperishable bliss."

Death is the mother of beauty; hence from her,

Alone, shall come fulfilment to our dreams

And our desires.   Although she strews the leaves

Of sure obliteration on our paths,

The path sick sorrow took, the many paths

Where triumph rang its brassy phrase, or love

Whispered a little out of tenderness,

She makes the willow shiver in the sun

For maidens who were wont to sit and gaze

Upon the grass, relinquished to their feet.

She causes boys to pile new plums and pears

On disregarded plate.   The maidens taste

And stray impassioned in the littering leaves.

VI

Is there no change of death in paradise ?

Does ripe fruit never fall ?   Or do the boughs

Hang always heavy in that perfect sky,

Unchanging, yet so like our perishing earth,

With rivers like our own that seek for seas

They never find, the same receding shores

That never touch with inarticulate pang ?

Why set the pear upon those river-banks

Or spice the shores with odors of the plum ?

Alas, that they should wear our colors there,

The silken weavings of our afternoons,

And pick the strings of our insipid lutes !
Death is the mother of beauty, mystical,
Within whose burning bosom we devise
Our earthly mothers waiting, sleeplessly.

VII

Supple and turbulent, a ring of men
Shall chant in orgy on a summer morn
Their boisterous devotion to the sun,
Not as a god, but as a god might be,
Naked among them, like a savage source.
Their chant shall be a chant of paradise,
Out of their blood, returning to the sky;
And in their chant shall enter, voice by voice,
The windy lake wherein their lord delights,
The trees, like serafin, and echoing hills,
That choir among themselves long afterward.
They shall know well the heavenly fellowship
Of men that perish and of summer morn.

And whence they came and whither they shall go
The dew upon their feet shall manifest.

VIII

She hears, upon that water without sound,
A voice that cries, "The tomb in Palestine
Is not the porch of spirits lingering.
It is the grave of Jesus, where he lay."
We live in an old chaos of the sun,
Or old dependency of day and night,
Or island solitude, unsponsored, free,
Of that wide water, inescapable.
Deer walk upon our mountains, and the quail
Whistle about us their spontaneous cries;
Sweet berries ripen in the wilderness;
And, in the isolation of the sky,
At evening, casual flocks of pigeons make
Ambiguous undulations as they sink,
Downward to darkness, on extended wings.

There are no bears among the roses,
Only a negress who supposes
Things false and wrong

About the lantern of the beauty
Who walks there, as a farewell duty,
Walks long and long.

The pity that her pious egress
Should fill the vigil of a negress
With heat so strong !

The lines are straight and swift between the stars.
The night is not the cradle that they cry,
The criers, undulating the deep-oceaned phrase.
The lines are much too dark and much too sharp.

The mind herein attains simplicity.
There is no moon, no single, silvered leaf.
The body is no body to be seen
But is an eye that studies its black lid.

Let these be your delight, secretive hunter,
Wading the sea-lines, moist and ever-mingling,
Mounting the earth-lines, long and lax, lethargic.
These lines are swift and fall without diverging.

121

The melon-flower nor dew nor web of either
Is like to these.   But in yourself is like:
A sheaf of brilliant arrows flying straight,
Flying and falling straightway for their pleasure,

Their pleasure that is all bright-edged and cold;
Or, if not arrows, then the nimblest motions,
Making recoveries of young nakedness
And the lost vehemence the midnights hold.

EXPLANATION

Ach, Mutter,
This old, black dress,
I have been embroidering
French flowers on it.

Not by way of romance,
Here is nothing of the ideal,
Nein,
Nein.

It would have been different,
Liebchen,
If I had imagined myself,
In an orange gown,
Drifting through space,
Like a figure on the church-wall.

I

An old man sits
In the shadow of a pine tree
In China.
He sees larkspur,
Blue and white,
At the edge of the shadow,
Move in the wind.
His beard moves in the wind.
The pine tree moves in the wind.
Thus water flows
Over weeds.

II

The night is of the color
Of a woman's arm:

Night, the female,

Obscure,

Fragrant and supple,

Conceals herself.

A pool shines,

Like a bracelet

Shaken in a dance.

III

I measure myself

Against a tall tree.

I find that I am much taller,

For I reach right up to the sun,

With my eye;

And I reach to the shore of the sea

With my ear.

Nevertheless, I dislike

The way the ants crawl

In and out of my shadow.

125

IV

When my dream was near the moon,
The white folds of its gown
Filled with yellow light.
The soles of its feet
Grew red.
Its hair filled
With certain blue crystallizations
From stars,
Not far off.

V

Not all the knives of the lamp-posts,
Nor the chisels of the long streets,
Nor the mallets of the domes
And high towers,
Can carve
What one star can carve,
Shining through the grape-leaves.

Rationalists, wearing square hats,

Think, in square rooms,

Looking at the floor,

Looking at the ceiling.

They confine themselves

To right-angled triangles.

If they tried rhomboids,

Cones, waving lines, ellipses —

As, for example, the ellipse of the half-moon —

Rationalists would wear sombreros.

Chieftain Iffucan of Azcan in caftan
Of tan with henna hackles, halt !

Damned universal cock, as if the sun
Was blackamoor to bear your blazing tail.

Fat ! Fat ! Fat ! Fat ! I am the personal.
Your world is you.   I am my world.

You ten-foot poet among inchlings. Fat !
Begone ! An inchling bristles in these pines,

Bristles, and points their Appalachian tangs,
And fears not portly Azcan nor his hoos.

I placed a jar in Tennessee,
And round it was, upon a hill.
It made the slovenly wilderness
Surround that hill.

The wilderness rose up to it,
And sprawled around, no longer wild.
The jar was round upon the ground
And tall and of a port in air.

It took dominion everywhere.
The jar was gray and bare.
It did not give of bird or bush,
Like nothing else in Tennessee.

The disbeliever walked the moonlit place,
Outside of gates of hammered serafin,
Observing the moon-blotches on the walls.

The yellow rocked across the still façades,
Or else sat spinning on the pinnacles,
While he imagined humming sounds and sleep.

The walker in the moonlight walked alone,
And each blank window of the building balked
His loneliness and what was in his mind:

If in a shimmering room the babies came,
Drawn close by dreams of fledgling wing,
It was because night nursed them in its fold.

Night nursed not him in whose dark mind
The clambering wings of birds of black revolved,
Making harsh torment of the solitude.

The walker in the moonlight walked alone,
And in his heart his disbelief lay cold.
His broad-brimmed hat came close upon his eyes.

FROGS EAT BUTTERFLIES. SNAKES EAT FROGS. HOGS EAT SNAKES. MEN EAT HOGS

It is true that the rivers went nosing like swine,
Tugging at banks, until they seemed
Bland belly-sounds in somnolent troughs,

That the air was heavy with the breath of these swine
The breath of turgid summer, and
Heavy with thunder's rattapallax,

That the man who erected this cabin, planted
This field, and tended it awhile,
Knew not the quirks of imagery,

That the hours of his indolent, arid days,
Grotesque with this nosing in banks,
This somnolence and rattapallax,

Seemed to suckle themselves on his arid being,

As the swine-like rivers suckled themselves

While they went seaward to the sea-mouths.

JASMINE'S BEAUTIFUL THOUGHTS
UNDERNEATH THE WILLOW

My titillations have no foot-notes
And their memorials are the phrases
Of idiosyncratic music.

The love that will not be transported
In an old, frizzled, flambeaued manner,
But muses on its eccentricity,

Is like a vivid apprehension
Of bliss beyond the mutes of plaster,
Or paper souvenirs of rapture,

Of bliss submerged beneath appearance,
In an interior ocean's rocking
Of long, capricious fugues and chorals.

Now, the wry Rosenbloom is dead
And his finical carriers tread,
On a hundred legs, the tread
Of the dead.
Rosenbloom is dead.

They carry the wizened one
Of the color of horn
To the sullen hill,
Treading a tread
In unison for the dead.

Rosenbloom is dead.
The tread of the carriers does not halt
On the hill, but turns
Up the sky.
They are bearing his body into the sky.

It is the infants of misanthropes

And the infants of nothingness

That tread

The wooden ascents

Of the ascending of the dead.

It is turbans they wear

And boots of fur

As they tread the boards

In a region of frost,

Viewing the frost;

To a chirr of gongs

And a chitter of cries

And the heavy thrum

Of the endless tread

That they tread;

To a jangle of doom

And a jumble of words

Of the intense poem

Of the strictest prose
Of Rosenbloom.

And they bury him there,
Body and soul,
In a place in the sky.
The lamentable tread !
Rosenbloom is dead.

TATTOO

The light is like a spider.
It crawls over the water.
It crawls over the edges of the snow.
It crawls under your eyelids
And spreads its webs there —
Its two webs.

The webs of your eyes
Are fastened
To the flesh and bones of you
As to rafters or grass.

There are filaments of your eyes
On the surface of the water
And in the edges of the snow.

THE BIRD WITH THE COPPERY,
KEEN CLAWS

Above the forest of the parakeets,
A parakeet of parakeets prevails,
A pip of life amid a mort of tails.

(The rudiments of tropics are around,
Aloe of ivory, pear of rusty rind.)
His lids are white because his eyes are blind.

He is not paradise of parakeets,
Of his gold ether, golden alguazil,
Except because he broods there and is still.

Panache upon panache, his tails deploy
Upward and outward, in green-vented forms,
His tip a drop of water full of storms.

But though the turbulent tinges undulate
As his pure intellect applies its laws,
He moves not on his coppery, keen claws.

He munches a dry shell while he exerts
His will, yet never ceases, perfect cock,
To flare, in the sun-pallor of his rock.

In Oklahoma,
Bonnie and Josie,
Dressed in calico,
Danced around a stump.
They cried,
"Ohoyaho,
Ohoo" . . .
Celebrating the marriage
Of flesh and air.

This is how the wind shifts:
Like the thoughts of an old human,
Who still thinks eagerly
And despairingly.
The wind shifts like this:
Like a human without illusions,
Who still feels irrational things within her.
The wind shifts like this:
Like humans approaching proudly,
Like humans approaching angrily.
This is how the wind shifts:
Like a human, heavy and heavy,
Who does not care.

COLLOQUY WITH A POLISH AUNT

*Elle savait toutes les légendes du Paradis et tous les contes
de la Pologne.*   — *Revue des Deux Mondes*

SHE

How is it that my saints from Voragine,

In their embroidered slippers, touch your spleen ?

HE

Old pantaloons, duenna of the spring !

SHE

Imagination is the will of things. . . .

Thus, on the basis of the common drudge,

You dream of women, swathed in indigo,

Holding their books toward the nearer stars,

To read, in secret, burning secrecies. . . .

That strange flower, the sun,

Is just what you say.

Have it your way.

The world is ugly,

And the people are sad.

That tuft of jungle feathers,

That animal eye,

Is just what you say.

That savage of fire,

That seed,

Have it your way.

The world is ugly,

And the people are sad.

TWO FIGURES IN DENSE
VIOLET NIGHT

I had as lief be embraced by the porter at the hotel
As to get no more from the moonlight
Than your moist hand.

Be the voice of night and Florida in my ear.
Use dusky words and dusky images.
Darken your speech.

Speak, even, as if I did not hear you speaking,
But spoke for you perfectly in my thoughts,
Conceiving words,

As the night conceives the sea-sounds in silence,
And out of their droning sibilants makes
A serenade.

145

Say, puerile, that the buzzards crouch on the ridge-pole
And sleep with one eye watching the stars fall
Below Key West.

Say that the palms are clear in a total blue,
Are clear and are obscure; that it is night;
That the moon shines.

THEORY

I am what is around me.

Women understand this.
One is not duchess
A hundred yards from a carriage.

These, then are portraits:
A black vestibule;
A high bed sheltered by curtains.

These are merely instances.

Sister and mother and diviner love,

And of the sisterhood of the living dead

Most near, most clear, and of the clearest bloom,

And of the fragrant mothers the most dear

And queen, and of diviner love the day

And flame and summer and sweet fire, no thread

Of cloudy silver sprinkles in your gown

Its venom of renown, and on your head

No crown is simpler than the simple hair.

Now, of the music summoned by the birth

That separates us from the wind and sea,

Yet leaves us in them, until earth becomes,

By being so much of the things we are,

Gross effigy and simulacrum, none

Gives motion to perfection more serene
Than yours, out of our imperfections wrought,
Most rare, or ever of more kindred air
In the laborious weaving that you wear.

For so retentive of themselves are men
That music is intensest which proclaims
The near, the clear, and vaunts the clearest bloom,
And of all vigils musing the obscure,
That apprehends the most which sees and names,
As in your name, an image that is sure,
Among the arrant spices of the sun,
O bough and bush and scented vine, in whom
We give ourselves our likest issuance.

Yet not too like, yet not so like to be
Too near, too clear, saving a little to endow
Our feigning with the strange unlike, whence springs
The difference that heavenly pity brings.
For this, musician, in your girdle fixed

Bear other perfumes.   On your pale head wear
A band entwining, set with fatal stones.
Unreal, give back to us what once you gave:
The imagination that we spurned and crave.

HYMN FROM A WATERMELON
PAVILION

You dweller in the dark cabin,
To whom the watermelon is always purple,
Whose garden is wind and moon,

Of the two dreams, night and day,
What lover, what dreamer, would choose
The one obscured by sleep ?

Here is the plantain by your door
And the best cock of red feather
That crew before the clocks.

A feme may come, leaf-green,
Whose coming may give revel
Beyond revelries of sleep,

Yes, and the blackbird spread its tail,
So that the sun may speckle,
While it creaks hail.

You dweller in the dark cabin,
Rise, since rising will not waken,
And hail, cry hail, cry hail.

I

Just as my fingers on these keys
Make music, so the selfsame sounds
On my spirit make a music, too.

Music is feeling, then, not sound;
And thus it is that what I feel,
Here in this room, desiring you,

Thinking of your blue-shadowed silk,
Is music.   It is like the strain
Waked in the elders by Susanna.

Of a green evening, clear and warm,
She bathed in her still garden, while
The red-eyed elders watching, felt

The basses of their beings throb
In witching chords, and their thin blood
Pulse pizzicati of Hosanna.

II

In the green water, clear and warm,
Susanna lay.
She searched
The touch of springs,
And found
Concealed imaginings.
She sighed,
For so much melody.

Upon the bank, she stood
In the cool
Of spent emotions.
She felt, among the leaves,
The dew
Of old devotions.

She walked upon the grass,
Still quavering.
The winds were like her maids,
On timid feet,
Fetching her woven scarves,
Yet wavering.

A breath upon her hand
Muted the night.
She turned —
A cymbal crashed,
And roaring horns.

III

Soon, with a noise like tambourines,
Came her attendant Byzantines.

They wondered why Susanna cried
Against the elders by her side;

And as they whispered, the refrain
Was like a willow swept by rain.

Anon, their lamps' uplifted flame
Revealed Susanna and her shame.

And then, the simpering Byzantines
Fled, with a noise like tambourines.

IV

Beauty is momentary in the mind —
The fitful tracing of a portal;
But in the flesh it is immortal.

The body dies; the body's beauty lives.
So evenings die, in their green going,
A wave, interminably flowing.
So gardens die, their meek breath scenting
The cowl of winter, done repenting.
So maidens die, to the auroral
Celebration of a maiden's choral.

Susanna's music touched the bawdy strings

Of those white elders; but, escaping,

Left only Death's ironic scraping.

Now, in its immortality, it plays

On the clear viol of her memory,

And makes a constant sacrament of praise.

THIRTEEN WAYS OF LOOKING AT A
BLACKBIRD

I

Among twenty snowy mountains,
The only moving thing
Was the eye of the blackbird.

II

I was of three minds,
Like a tree
In which there are three blackbirds.

III

The blackbird whirled in the autumn winds.
It was a small part of the pantomime.

IV

A man and a woman
Are one.
A man and a woman and a blackbird
Are one.

V

I do not know which to prefer,
The beauty of inflections
Or the beauty of innuendoes,
The blackbird whistling
Or just after.

VI

Icicles filled the long window
With barbaric glass.
The shadow of the blackbird
Crossed it, to and fro.
The mood
Traced in the shadow
An indecipherable cause.

159

VII

O thin men of Haddam,
Why do you imagine golden birds ?
Do you not see how the blackbird
Walks around the feet
Of the women about you ?

VIII

I know noble accents
And lucid, inescapable rhythms;
But I know, too,
That the blackbird is involved
In what I know.

IX

When the blackbird flew out of sight,
It marked the edge
Of one of many circles.

X

At the sight of blackbirds
Flying in a green light,
Even the bawds of euphony
Would cry out sharply.

XI

He rode over Connecticut
In a glass coach.
Once, a fear pierced him,
In that he mistook
The shadow of his equipage
For blackbirds.

XII

The river is moving.
The blackbird must be flying.

XIII

It was evening all afternoon.
It was snowing

And it was going to snow.
The blackbird sat
In the cedar-limbs.

As the immense dew of Florida
Brings forth
The big-finned palm
And green vine angering for life,

As the immense dew of Florida
Brings forth hymn and hymn
From the beholder,
Beholding all these green sides
And gold sides of green sides,

And blessed mornings,
Meet for the eye of the young alligator,
And lightning colors
So, in me, come flinging
Forms, flames, and the flakes of flames.

The time of year has grown indifferent.
Mildew of summer and the deepening snow
Are both alike in the routine I know.
I am too dumbly in my being pent.

The wind attendant on the solstices
Blows on the shutters of the metropoles,
Stirring no poet in his sleep, and tolls
The grand ideas of the villages.

The malady of the quotidian. . . .
Perhaps, if winter once could penetrate
Through all its purples to the final slate,
Persisting bleakly in an icy haze,

One might in turn become less diffident,

Out of such mildew plucking neater mould

And spouting new orations of the cold.

One might.   One might.   But time will not relent.

Life contracts and death is expected,
As in a season of autumn.
The soldier falls.

He does not become a three-days personage,
Imposing his separation,
Calling for pomp.

Death is absolute and without memorial,
As in a season of autumn,
When the wind stops,

When the wind stops and, over the heavens,
The clouds go, nevertheless,
In their direction.

Hi !   The creator too is blind,
Struggling toward his harmonious whole,
Rejecting intermediate parts,
Horrors and falsities and wrongs;
Incapable master of all force,
Too vague idealist, overwhelmed
By an afflatus that persists.
For this, then, we endure brief lives,
The evanescent symmetries
From that meticulous potter's thumb.

THE SURPRISES OF THE
SUPERHUMAN

The palais de justice of chambermaids
Tops the horizon with its colonnades.

If it were lost in Übermenschlichkeit,
Perhaps our wretched state would soon come right.

For somehow the brave dicta of its kings
Make more awry our faulty human things.

SEA SURFACE FULL OF CLOUDS

I

In that November off Tehuantepec,
The slopping of the sea grew still one night
And in the morning summer hued the deck

And made one think of rosy chocolate
And gilt umbrellas. Paradisal green
Gave suavity to the perplexed machine

Of ocean, which like limpid water lay.
Who, then, in that ambrosial latitude
Out of the light evolved the moving blooms,

Who, then, evolved the sea-blooms from the clouds
Diffusing balm in that Pacific calm ?
C'était mon enfant, mon bijou, mon âme.

The sea-clouds whitened far below the calm
And moved, as blooms move, in the swimming green
And in its watery radiance, while the hue

Of heaven in an antique reflection rolled
Round those flotillas.   And sometimes the sea
Poured brilliant iris on the glistening blue.

II

In that November off Tehuantepec
The slopping of the sea grew still one night.
At breakfast jelly yellow streaked the deck

And made one think of chop-house chocolate
And sham umbrellas.   And a sham-like green
Capped summer-seeming on the tense machine

Of ocean, which in sinister flatness lay.
Who, then, beheld the rising of the clouds
That strode submerged in that malevolent sheen,

170

Who saw the mortal massives of the blooms
Of water moving on the water-floor ?
C'était mon frère du ciel, ma vie, mon or.

The gongs rang loudly as the windy booms
Hoo-hooed it in the darkened ocean-blooms.
The gongs grew still.   And then blue heaven spread

Its crystalline pendentives on the sea
And the macabre of the water-glooms
In an enormous undulation fled.

III

In that November off Tehuantepec,
The slopping of the sea grew still one night
And a pale silver patterned on the deck

And made one think of porcelain chocolate
And pied umbrellas.   An uncertain green,
Piano-polished, held the tranced machine

171

Of ocean, as a prelude holds and holds.

Who, seeing silver petals of white blooms

Unfolding in the water, feeling sure

Of the milk within the saltiest spurge, heard, then,

The sea unfolding in the sunken clouds?

Oh! C'était mon extase et mon amour.

So deeply sunken were they that the shrouds,

The shrouding shadows, made the petals black

Until the rolling heaven made them blue,

A blue beyond the rainy hyacinth,

And smiting the crevasses of the leaves

Deluged the ocean with a sapphire blue.

IV

In that November off Tehuantepec

The night-long slopping of the sea grew still.

A mallow morning dozed upon the deck

And made one think of musky chocolate
And frail umbrellas.   A too-fluent green
Suggested malice in the dry machine

Of ocean, pondering dank stratagem.
Who then beheld the figures of the clouds
Like blooms secluded in the thick marine?

Like blooms?   Like damasks that were shaken off
From the loosed girdles in the spangling must.
C'était ma foi, la nonchalance divine.

The nakedness would rise and suddenly turn
Salt masks of beard and mouths of bellowing,
Would — But more suddenly the heaven rolled

Its bluest sea-clouds in the thinking green,
And the nakedness became the broadest blooms,
Mile-mallows that a mallow sun cajoled.

In that November off Tehuantepec
Night stilled the slopping of the sea.   The day
Came, bowing and voluble, upon the deck,

Good clown. . . . One thought of Chinese chocolate
And large umbrellas.   And a motley green
Followed the drift of the obese machine

Of ocean, perfected in indolence.
What pistache one, ingenious and droll,
Beheld the sovereign clouds as jugglery

And the sea as turquoise-turbaned Sambo, neat
At tossing saucers — cloudy-conjuring sea?
C'était mon esprit bâtard, l'ignominie.

The sovereign clouds came clustering.   The conch
Of loyal conjuration trumped.   The wind
Of green blooms turning crisped the motley hue

To clearing opalescence.   Then the sea
And heaven rolled as one and from the two
Came fresh transfigurings of freshest blue.

THE REVOLUTIONISTS STOP FOR
ORANGEADE

Capitán profundo, capitán geloso,
Ask us not to sing standing in the sun,
Hairy-backed and hump-armed,
Flat-ribbed and big-bagged.
There is no pith in music
Except in something false.

Bellissimo, pomposo,
Sing a song of serpent-kin,
Necks among the thousand leaves,
Tongues around the fruit.
Sing in clownish boots
Strapped and buckled bright.

Wear the breeches of a mask,
Coat half-flare and half galloon;
Wear a helmet without reason,
Tufted, tilted, twirled, and twisted.
Start the singing in a voice
Rougher than a grinding shale.

Hang a feather by your eye,
Nod and look a little sly.
This must be the vent of pity,
Deeper than a truer ditty
Of the real that wrenches,
Of the quick that's wry.

I

The Whole World Including the Speaker

Why nag at the ideas of Hercules, Don Don ?
Widen your sense.   All things in the sun are sun.

II

The Whole World Excluding the Speaker

I found between moon-rising and moon-setting
The world was round.   But not from my begetting.

III

Soupe Aux Perles

Health-o, when ginger and fromage bewitch
The vile antithesis of poor and rich.

178

IV

Soupe Sans Perles

I crossed in '38 in the *Western Head.*
It depends which way you crossed, the tea-belle said.

V

Boston With a Note-book

Lean encyclopædists, inscribe an Iliad.
There's a weltanschauung of the penny pad.

VI

Boston Without a Note-book

Let us erect in the Basin a lofty fountain.
Suckled on ponds, the spirit craves a watery mountain.

VII

Artist in Tropic

Of Phœbus Apothicaire the first beatitude:
Blessed, who is his nation's multitude.

VIII

Artist in Arctic

And of Phœbus the Tailor the second saying goes:
Blessed, whose beard is cloak against the snows.

IX

Statue against a Clear Sky

Ashen man on ashen cliff above the salt halloo,
O ashen admiral of the hale, hard blue. . . .

X

Statue against a Cloudy Sky

Scaffolds and derricks rise from the reeds to the clouds
Meditating the will of men in formless crowds.

XI

Land of Locust

Patron and patriarch of couplets, walk
In fragrant leaves heat-heavy yet nimble in talk.

XII

Land of Pine and Marble

Civilization must be destroyed.   The hairy saints
Of the North have earned this crumb by their com-
  plaints.

XIII

The Male Nude

Dark cynic, strip and bathe and bask at will.
Without cap or strap, you are the cynic still.

XIV

The Female Nude

Ballatta dozed in the cool on a straw divan
At home, a bit like the slenderest courtesan.

XV

Scène Flétrie

The purple dress in autumn and the belfry breath
Hinted autumnal farewells of academic death.

XVI

Scène Fleurie

A perfect fruit in perfect atmosphere.

Nature as Pinakothek.   Whist !   Chanticleer. . . .

LUNAR PARAPHRASE

The moon is the mother of pathos and pity.

When, at the wearier end of November,
Her old light moves along the branches,
Feebly, slowly, depending upon them;
When the body of Jesus hangs in a pallor,
Humanly near, and the figure of Mary,
Touched on by hoar-frost, shrinks in a shelter
Made by the leaves, that have rotted and fallen;
When over the houses, a golden illusion
Brings back an earlier season of quiet
And quieting dreams in the sleepers in darkness —

The moon is the mother of pathos and pity.

I

If from the earth we came, it was an earth
That bore us as a part of all the things
It breeds and that was lewder than it is.
Our nature is her nature.   Hence it comes,
Since by our nature we grow old, earth grows
The same.   We parallel the mother's death.
She walks an autumn ampler than the wind
Cries up for us and colder than the frost
Pricks in our spirits at the summer's end,
And over the bare spaces of our skies
She sees a barer sky that does not bend.

II

The body walks forth naked in the sun
And, out of tenderness or grief, the sun

Gives comfort, so that other bodies come,

Twinning our phantasy and our device,

And apt in versatile motion, touch and sound

To make the body covetous in desire

Of the still finer, more implacable chords.

So be it.   Yet the spaciousness and light

In which the body walks and is deceived,

Falls from that fatal and that barer sky,

And this the spirit sees and is aggrieved.

A slash of angular blacks
Like a fractured edifice
That was buttressed by blue slants
In a coma of the moon.

A slash and the edifice fell,
Pylon and pier fell down.
A mountain-blue cloud arose
Like a thing in which they fell,

Fell slowly as when at night
A languid janitor bears
His lantern through colonnades
And the architecture swoons.

It turned cold and silent.   Then

The square began to clear.

The bijou of Atlas, the moon,

Was last with its porcelain leer.

If any duck in any brook,
Fluttering the water
For your crumb,
Seemed the helpless daughter

Of a mother
Regretful that she bore her;
Or of another,
Barren, and longing for her;

What of the dove,
Or thrush, or any singing mysteries?
What of the trees
And intonations of the trees?

What of the night

That lights and dims the stars?

Do you know, Hans Christian,

Now that you see the night?

The mountains between our lands and the sea —
This conjunction of mountains and sea and our lands —
Have I stopped and thought of its point before ?

When I think of our lands I think of the house
And the table that holds a platter of pears,
Vermilion smeared over green, arranged for show.

But this gross blue under rolling bronzes
Belittles those carefully chosen daubs.
Flashier fruits !   A flip for the sun and moon,

If they mean no more than that.   But they do.
And mountains and the sea do.   And our lands.
And the welter of frost and the fox cries do.

Much more than that.   Autumnal passages
Are overhung by the shadows of the rocks
And his nostrils blow out salt around each man.

Mow the grass in the cemetery, darkies,
Study the symbols and the requiescats,
But leave a bed beneath the myrtles.
This skeleton had a daughter and that, a son.

In his time, this one had little to speak of,
The softest word went gurrituck in his skull.
For him the moon was always in Scandinavia
And his daughter was a foreign thing.

And that one was never a man of heart.
The making of his son was one more duty.
When the music of the boy fell like a fountain,
He praised Johann Sebastian, as he should.

The dark shadows of the funereal magnolias

Are full of the songs of Jamanda and Carlotta;

The son and the daughter, who come to the darkness,

He for her burning breast and she for his arms.

And these two never meet in the air so full of summer

And touch each other, even touching closely,

Without an escape in the lapses of their kisses.

Make a bed and leave the iris in it.

The trade-wind jingles the rings in the nets around the
racks by the docks on Indian River.
It is the same jingle of the water among the roots under
the banks of the palmettoes,
It is the same jingle of the red-bird breasting the orange-
trees out of the cedars.
Yet there is no spring in Florida, neither in boskage
perdu, nor on the nunnery beaches.

TEA

When the elephant's-ear in the park
Shrivelled in frost,
And the leaves on the paths
Ran like rats,
Your lamp-light fell
On shining pillows,
Of sea-shades and sky-shades,
Like umbrellas in Java.

What syllable are you seeking,

Vocalissimus,

In the distances of sleep ?

Speak it.

A NOTE ON THE TYPE IN WHICH
THIS BOOK IS SET

This book was set on the Linotype in Janson, a recutting made direct from the type cast from matrices made by Anton Janson some time between 1660 and 1687.

Of Janson's origin nothing is known. He may have been a relative of Justus Janson, a printer of Danish birth who practiced in Leipzig from 1614 to 1635. Some time between 1657 and 1668 Anton Janson, a punchcutter and type-founder, bought from the Leipzig printer Johann Erich Hahn the type-foundry which had formerly been a part of the printing house of M. Friedrich Lankisch. Janson's types were first shown in a specimen sheet issued at Leipzig about 1675.

The book was composed, printed, and bound by The Plimpton Press, Norwood, Massachusetts. Typography and binding based on original designs by W. A. Dwiggins.